Diary of a Pastor's Wife

"Wings of God's Presence"

Diary of a Pastor's Wife

"Wings of God's Presence"

by

Moira Boakai

*"He will cover you with His feathers,
and under His wings you will find refuge;
His faithfulness will be your shield and
rampart."*
Psalm 91:4

Anointed Rose Press Publishing™

Anointed Rose Press™

DIARY OF A PASTOR'S WIFE©
- Wings of God's Presence -

Copyright©2025 by Moira Boakai

PHONE: 1(302)561-0963
EMAIL: moira.boakai@gmail.com

Diary of A Pastor's Wife / Moira Boakai
(trade paperback: alkaline paper)

ISBN 13:979-8-9993069-3-7
LCCN: 2025914880

Personal Memoirs / Family Relationships

Cover Designed by September Summer
Publisher: Anointed Rose Press
Email: septembersummer09@gmail.com
1(484)378-0939

Scripture quotations taken from the Holy Bible, New International Version®, NIV®. Copyright © by Biblica, Inc.® Used by permission. All rights reserved worldwide.

PRINTED IN THE USA

// TABLE OF CONTENTS

PART:

DEDICATION

This book is lovingly dedicated to my children.

You are my living testimony of God's faithfulness and grace.

May your wings never be clipped and your spirits never broken.

— *Moira Boakai*

// ACKNOWLEDGMENT

First, I give all glory to God for being my refuge and strength through every season of this story.

To my beautiful children Shalom, Ade'e and Lelah, and my handsome grandson Adaan…thank you for never giving up on me.

To my dear friend Karen DeGrasse, your prayers and unwavering support have lifted me higher than you know.

May every reader find healing, hope, and courage to break free.

...Moira Boakai

// FOREWORD

I've had the honor of walking beside Moira Boakai through some of the darkest and most painful, and yet most powerful seasons of her life. I watched her stand when she had every reason to collapse. I listened to her cry prayers that no one else heard. I witnessed her fight for her children, her faith, and herself—with a strength that could only have come from God.

"Diary of a Pastor's Wife" is not just a story—it's a lifeline. It's the voice of a woman who was expected to stay silent. It's the truth behind the smile so many saw on Sundays. It's the raw, unfiltered reality of a life that looked polished on the outside, but was unraveling behind closed doors.

Moira doesn't write this to blame. She writes it to heal—and to help others heal too. Her words carry weight because they were birthed in pain, but they also carry hope because they are drenched in grace.

This book will speak to the heart of every woman who has ever felt trapped in a role she didn't choose, silenced by expectations, or broken by someone who should have protected her. It will challenge the church to look again—closer, deeper, and with more compassion. And it will remind every reader that even in the most desperate moments, God is still writing a beautiful story.

Moira's courage inspires me every single day. And I pray that as you turn each page, you'll see not just her journey—but your own reflection in the light of redemption.

She broke free. And so can you.

—Karen DeGrasse

Friend

// PREFACE

As you hold this book in your hands, I pray you feel the same hope that carried me through some of my darkest days. "The Diary of a Pastor's Wife" is not just my story — it's a glimpse into the silent prayers, hidden tears, and quiet strength that so many of us carry when no one is watching.

For years, I wore a smile while my heart ached behind closed doors. But through it all, God was faithful. He heard every whispered prayer and bottled every tear. Writing these pages has been a journey of healing for me, and my deepest desire is that as you turn each one, you find your own courage to stand, to heal, and to know that you are never alone.

May my story remind you that even when life feels unbearable, there is hope beyond the pain and restoration waiting on the other side of surrender.

Thank you for walking this road with me. May you find comfort beneath His wings.

With love and faith,

...Moira Boakai

// INTRODUCTION

This is a deeply personal and inspirational memoir, capturing my journey from childhood into adulthood, including struggles in Liberia which were survived through resilience, faith, and triumph. A compelling narrative, told with depth, emotion, and reflection with powerful themes of perseverance, faith, and transformation.

This book, "Diary of A Pastor's Wife ", was birthed in the small West African country of Liberia. I was born to a single mother who had me at the age of 14. My mother was a strong, hard-working, and courageous woman, well known in the community for her public service work. When she had me, she had no idea how to care for a child, so her aunt, with whom she was living at the time, helped raise me.

My father was initially nowhere to be found, just like some typical African men who impregnate young girls and then walk away. Eventually, my father resurfaced. At one point, in anger he decided to place a curse on me, saying that I would be nothing, that I wouldn't be worthy…that I would be a prostitute.

This book walks through my childhood, with its multiple challenges and traumatic experiences, through my teen years including survival through the horrific Liberian Civil War, and into my adulthood when I married the one who promised me so much…

//PART ONE:

Our Beginnings in Liberia

My mother, Naomi, was born and raised in Liberia, where she lived with her family up until the age of 14. As the oldest of her siblings, she carried a heavy load of responsibility from a young age…always helping, always putting others before herself.

Her father, my grandfather, was a Muslim who had migrated from another part of Liberia and settled in a new city. It was there he met my grandmother, and together they built a life and raised their children. My mother was their firstborn, and with that came the expectation to help care for her younger brothers and sisters. She never had much of a childhood. She was always the one everyone depended on.

When things became difficult at home, my mother went to live with her aunt - Aunt Lucy. Aunt Lucy wasn't just any relative; she was my grandmother's sister. She became a strong, guiding force in both my mother's life and later in mine.

She helped raise my mom during her teenage years, and after I was born, she was the one who stepped in to help raise me too. Aunt Lucy was love, strength, and stability all in one. Her presence shaped both my mother and myself in ways I'm still grateful for to this day. My mother's resilience and public service also shaped my view of strength and perseverance.

On a bustling street of Granga, a Liberian City, fourteen-year-old Naomi's Auntie Lucy is preparing to alight from a luxury ride. The side window winds down, and she bends to give her boyfriend Sam a peck, when suddenly a small boy snatches her handbag and dashes away.

Sam started chasing him and the cab driver jumped out of the car to chase him, yelling, "Thief! Thief! Thief!" The boy disappeared into an alley.

Auntie Lucy also begins chasing the boy, while screaming loudly, "Somebody, somebody please catch him. He snatched my handbag!" She eventually stopped running as the boy is too fast, and she saw him almost hit by the traffic while dodging through it.

The driver was now standing there dazed, looking at the thief as he disappeared into another alley. He stood shaking his head and muttering to himself, "He's very agile and smart. He should be competing in the Olympics. What a waste of talent."

Aunt Lucy pulled Sam's hand gently to get his attention, while complaining loudly and expressing her frustration. "He took my handbag. Everything you gave me is inside that bag. I am going to die of heartbreak." She then fell into his arms while crying on his chest.

Sam tried to comfort her, "Oh dear, that's very serious, but don't worry about it. I'll give you double whatever he took from you. Count it as a blessing in disguise."

Aunt Lucy said, "Oh my God! Really?" while gently pushing him a little space away from her to get a good look at his face, while he is smiling. "Thank you so much my Prince with a shiny armor." she exclaims, while jumping back into his arms like a little girl that has just been given a cup of delicious ice cream. She keeps her gaze on him steadily.

"Why are you looking at me like that?" Sam asked. "Is that not enough? Do you want me to triple the gift?"

Auntie gushed, "You are too kind. You enjoy making me happy, that's why I'm always thinking about you. Whenever I am with you, I forget all my worries."

"It's your joy," Sam replied, "the joy you express every time you are with me; that's my motivation. As long as you are happy to be mine, I'll not leave you alone."

Auntie is feeling very happy, "Can I ask you something?"

Sam said, "Go ahead."

"I am just curious, are all men as kind and as generous as you?"

"Well, I think my people are generally hospitable, kind and generous by nature. So, yes, in a way all men should be kind people."

While looking straight into his eyes Auntie cooed, "In that case take me with you. I want to follow you to your country. I want to experience the kindness and generosity of your people for the rest of my life."

Fourteen-year-old Naomi is daydreaming with her mind drifting to an earlier time in her life when she was eight years old. Away from the city of Granga, a cab pulled up to the local street where Auntie Lucy lives. The driver said, "We are here Ma. I hope you enjoyed my fast but safe driving."

"Sure, you are a smart driver," Auntie says as she pays him, opens the car and steps out of the car into the active and lively street. She's carrying some shopping bags as she strolls majestically towards her house.

Naomi sights her Auntie from a distance and screams joyfully as she runs to meet her. Auntie Lucy stops and stands with her arms spread wide in anticipation of young Naomi's embrace.

Naomi's thoughts return to the present when she is more mature and engaged in community service. She's just rounding up helping an aged woman clean up her surroundings.

"Mama, I have finished with the cleaning. Your laundry is done and everywhere is now clean and hygienic. I'll come again by the weekend to check on how you're doing. Okay?"

Auntie smiled, "Thank you my daughter. Your mother has raised a good child. I pray for you that God will send to you His angels to also help you in the times of your need."

"A big 'Amen' Mama, thank you for your kind thoughts towards your humble child."

While Naomi is on her way to school, she stops over to see Luciano. While knocking at the door, her face is brimming with smiles.

After a short while, the door creaks open and Luciano pops his face through. "Ooh! Hello, my beautiful angel. Wow! You are looking more and more angelic every day. Come in, come in."

Naomi hesitated a little, "You know I have to be on my way to school, right? So, we can't do anything right now," she said shyly.

He replied, "Of course my little angel. Yesterday was extraordinary. Though I am so hungry for more, I understand your education is for the best of both of our futures together."

"That's nice," Naomi giggled, "I am happy you still think that my getting a proper education is good for us. Every day, I keep creaming of all your wonderful promises to me."

"Really, you mean you are seriously thinking about my promises to you, and the big dreams I dream for both of us?"

"Luciano, of course I do. Why shouldn't I. Your promises are like sweet melody to my soul. Those dreams are what made me believe you really love me. And that's why I released myself to you."

"My angel that's a beautiful thing to say to me. So, you trust me now completely because of the promises?"

She laughed, "Yes! I know you'll never disappoint me."

"Disappoint? How can I do such a horrible thing to you. Don't worry about anything; for as long as you keep loving me, I'll will treat you as my queen." He steps back inside momentarily and returns with some money and gives it to her. "Buy yourself something nice and tasty at school. Make sure you come back here quickly after school, before going home. Okay?"

"Okay, Naomi replies, smiling shyly, "so you mean you enjoy my company always?"

"Of course I do. You are always fun to be with!" He noticed the idea pleased her, so he praised her more, flattering her.

"Really!" she exclaimed excitedly, "stop flattering me big man. You're making me shy." She hits him playfully and runs away.

"My little sweet butterfly. I'll be right here waiting for you, sugar pie. Make sure you come back quickly."

>>>>>>>>.

While Naomi is standing with her best friend Abigail under a tree, Abigail is looking her over. "Naomi, my sweet friend, have you noticed that you are changing? You are glowing. What am I missing?"

Naomi gushes, "I don't know what is going on in the inside of me, but I feel like I am literally blooming. But I've been feeling like I want to throw up more often recently."

Eyeing her suspiciously, Abigail says, "I hope what I'm thinking is not true. Have you eaten the forbidden fruit?"

"Which forbidden fruit did I eat? What are you talking about? Please stop speaking nonsense," Naomi hits her friend tenderly, suddenly feeling shy and guilty all at once.

Abigail gently said, "Hmm. I just hope you're not...because you would have just thrown our dreams of a great future together into the trash can."

>>>>>>>>>>>>

Naomi sits on a small stool in Auntie Lucy's modestly furnished living room, looking pale and her eyes are red from crying.

Auntie Lucy paces back and forth, with her arms crossed, and a mixture of anger and concern on her face. "I warned you, Naomi! I told you to be careful with that boy, Luciano. Men like him...they whisper sweet words until they get what they want, then they disappear like smoke. And you, you wouldn't listen!"

With a trembling voice, Naomi cried, "I know, Auntie! I know. I was foolish. He... he made so many promises. I thought he loved me."

No longer pacing, and while looking at Naomi, Auntie's expression softened slightly. "Love? Child, what do you know about love at your age? He preyed on your innocence, but crying won't change what has been done."

Sighing heavily and sitting beside Naomi, while putting an arm around her shoulder, Auntie said, "Now, now. Stop your weeping. It's not the end of the world, though it feels like it, I know."

Leaning into Auntie, with fresh tears welling up, Naomi cried, "What am I going to do, Auntie? I...I am pregnant."

Nodding slowly, with a grim look on her face, Auntie said, "I suspected as much. You've had that look about you for weeks."

Holding Naomi tighter for a moment, then pulling back slightly to look her in the eyes, Auntie said, "First, you must tell him. He has a responsibility in this. You must go and see Luciano. Tell him he is going to be a father."

Wiping her eyes, with a flicker of determination appearing, Naomi said, "Yes, Auntie. I will. I have to. He needs to know. Maybe... maybe he'll do the right thing."

Scoffing softly, "Maybe, but don't build your hopes too high, child. Men can be cowards. But you must face him. You are stronger than you think."

Naomi nods, taking a deep breath, "I... I'll go today," while Auntie Lucy gives her a supportive squeeze. Naomi looks a little more composed, but the fear is still in her eyes.

Naomi stands nervously outside Luciano's small, somewhat unkempt house. The paint is peeling, and the yard is overgrown. She takes a deep breath and knocks on the door.

After a moment, Luciano opens the door. He looked surprised, then annoyed to see her. "Naomi? What are you doing here? I told you not to come unannounced."

With a small but firm voice, Naomi said, "Luciano, we need to talk. It's important."

Leaning against the door frame, looking impatient, he says, "I'm busy. Make it quick."

Taking a deep breath, with her heart pounding, "Luciano, I'm pregnant. It's yours."

Luciano's eyes widen for a split second, then his expression turns cold and dismissive. He laughs...a harsh, cruel sound. "Pregnant? And you think it's mine? Don't be ridiculous, girl. How many others have you been with? You think you can pin this on me?"

Shocked, with tears springing to her eyes, Naomi cried, "What? How can you say that? You know there's been no one else! You said you loved me! You promised..."

"Promises?" scoffingly he said, "you girls are all the same. You hear what you want to hear. I don't have time for this drama. I'm not responsible for your mistakes. Now, get out of here." He starts to close the door.

Desperate and reaching out she begged, "Luciano, please! Don't do this to me! What about our future? What about the baby?"

He pushes her hand away, hardening his face. "There is no 'our' future, and there is no 'our' baby. That's your problem, not mine." as he slams the door in her face. The sound echoes in the quiet street.

Naomi stands there, stunned, tears streaming down her face, as her body trembles. Slowly, as if her legs can no longer support her, she sinks to the dusty pavement in front of the house. She curls into a ball, her shoulders shaking with violent sobs, the picture of utter devastation and abandonment. She had no idea how to carry a pregnancy or take care of a child. My father was the very first man in her life, and after that, she became pregnant right away

Naomi is sitting on the edge of the single bed in the room of Nora, Abigail's sister, with her face tear-stained and swollen. Abigail, the same age as Naomi, sits beside her, holding her hand, her own eyes filled with sympathy.

Abigail spoke softly, "Oh, Naomi. I can't believe he would do that, after everything he said to you, after everything you shared. He's a monster."

Naomi's voice choked with sobs, "He just... he just slammed the door. He said it wasn't his. He said I was... (She can't bring herself to repeat his accusations). He's gone, Abigail. He just left me, like I was nothing."

Abigail pulls Naomi into a hug, rocking her gently, "Shhh, shhh. You are not nothing, Naomi.

You hear me? You are strong, and you are good. He is the one who is worthless. He's a coward."

Clinging to Abigail, Naomi cries out, "But what am I going to do? I'm pregnant, and he... he has disappeared. My auntie was right. I was so stupid."

Abigail pulls back slightly to look at Naomi, her expression earnest, "You weren't stupid, Naomi. You were in love, or you thought you were. He tricked you. It's not your fault. And you're not alone. You have your Auntie, and you have me. We'll face this together."

Looking at Abigail, a glimmer of hope came to Naomi's tear-filled eyes. "You really mean that?

Nodding firmly, she squeezes Naomi's hand, "Of course, I do. We are friends, aren't we? Best friends. We'll figure something out. It will be hard, I know, but we'll find a way. You won't go through this alone."

Naomi manages a weak, watery smile. She leans her head on Abigail's shoulder, finding a small measure of comfort in her friend's unwavering support. The two girls sit together in silence for a while, with a shared sorrow and a budding resolve filling the small room.

Naomi's mind wanders to the past again to her eight-year-old self, seated in front of Abigail's and Nora's house as they talk about their future ambitions and education. They are holding a little school pamphlet about a nursing career.

With her eyes shining with excitement, Abigail gushed, "Imagine, Naomi! Once you finish your schooling and become a proper nurse, with that healing touch of yours, you'll be able to help so many people. And you promised, remember? You promised you'd come back for me."

Smiling confidently, Naomi replied, "Of course, I remember, Nora! How could I forget? We are a team. I'll become the best nurse in Liberia, and then I 'll make sure you get your chance too. We'll show everyone what we can do."

Abigail sighs contentedly, "It's going to be wonderful. No more struggling. We'll have our own lives and make our own way. Your education is the key, Naomi. It will open all the doors for us."

Nodding with her face alight with determination, Naomi replied, "It will Abi. I'll work hard. For both of us. We'll have a future so bright, it'll blind everyone who doubted us."

They both laugh...a carefree, joyful sound, full of the optimism and hopefulness of youth.

Naomi has another memory, one of herself and Abigail walking through a bustling schoolyard, perhaps during a break. They are animatedly discussing their future plans; their voices filled with ambition.

Naomi says excitingly, "Abigail, after I get my nursing degree, we'll save up. We'll both go abroad - maybe to America or England! We'll become graduate nurses, the best of the best."

With eyes wide with wonder, Abigail said, "Abroad? Do you really think we could. Naomi? It seems like such a faraway dream."

Naomi stops walking and turns to Abigail, her expression serious but inspiring – "Dreams are only faraway if you don't chase them, Abigail. We'll chase this one together. And when we come back, we won't just work in any hospital. We'll open our own private clinic, right here, in our community."

With awe in her voice, Abigail gushes, "Our own clinic? To help our own people? Oh, Naomi, that would be...that would be everything."

Grinning, "Abi, exactly! We'll provide the best care. We'll make a real difference. No one will have to suffer because they can't afford help. It will be our legacy."

They link arms, their steps light and purposeful, walking towards a future they believe is within their grasp. The sun shines brightly on them.

Presently, Naomi and Abigail are sitting in front of Abigail's house, holding each other, the weight of Naomi's current reality crushing them both.

With her voice thick with tears, and shaking her head, Naomi grieved, "Just one wrong misstep, one moment of weakness, and everything, everything we dreamed of ..."

Sobbing into Abigail's shoulder, she cried, "It's all gone, Abigail! Gone! Like it was never even there! All those plans, all those promises!"

She pulls back, her face a mask of anguish, looking at Abigail desperately. "Oh, how easily and quickly can great and big dreams fade away! With just one wrong step!"

They are both crying openly now, like lost children. The shared grief is palpable. They hold onto each other as if they are the only two people in a vast, unforgiving wilderness, with their dreams shattered around them.

Whispering, Naomi says hoarsely, "It's not fair. It's just not fair;" as she looks around the room, as if seeing the ghosts of their past hopes.

"We were going to conquer the world Abi - remember?"

Abigail nods, unable to speak through her tears. They look at each other's grief-stricken faces, the dreams of the past now a painful memory.

Naomi finds herself in a flower field moving with a light, almost giddy step. Her face reflects a sense of new, exhilarating emotion. She touches the petals of a flower, a small, secretive smile on her lips.

The feeling is one of a beautiful butterfly, flitting from one bloom to another, intoxicated by the nectar of a new, forbidden experience.

There's an innocence to her joy, but also a hint of the recklessness that will lead to her current predicament. Suddenly she is stung by an insect, and she lets out a painful yell.

Suddenly, she jerks out of her sleep with a yell, and finds herself inside her small, simple room.

"Heh!" she mutters as she looks thoughtful, and a little troubled, as she looks ahead).

Naomi remembers the faint echo of Abigail's warning, as she has a flashback of their previous conversation:

Abigail, who is looking her over said, "My sweet friend, have you noticed that you are changing? You are glowing. What am I missing?"

Naomi replied, "I don't know what is going on in the inside of me, but I feel like I am literally blooming. But I've been feeling like I want to throw up more often recently.'

Abigail eyes her suspiciously, "I hope what I am thinking is not true. Have you eaten the forbidden fruit?

"Which forbidden fruit did I eat?" Naomi said, "what are you talking about? Please stop speaking nonsense." as she hits her friend tenderly, suddenly feeling shy and guilty all at once.

Abigail says, "Hmm. I just hope you're not, because you would have just thrown our dreams of a great future together into the trash can.

Back in the present, Naomi lets out a heavy loud sigh and drops her head. As she raises her head again, tears run down her eyes, and she stares ahead.

Abigail sits in front of her house looking ahead in deep quiet thought. After a while, she shakes her head and lets out a loud hiss. "Our dreams, they had wings, Naomi's and mine. We thought they'd carry us so high. But now they've flown away. And I don't think they're coming back."

She looks down at her hands, clenching them, while a new, harder expression settles on her face. Hope is gone, replaced by grim pragmatism. "I can't keep waiting for dreams that are dead. Hope... hope is a luxury I can't afford anymore. That older man, the one who keeps pestering my family because of me. He's rich. He can offer a roof over my head. Food. Clothes. It's not the life I wanted. It's not love. But it's something. It's survival." She shudders slightly but her resolve hardens as she rises from where she is seated and walks into the house.

Naomi, now visibly pregnant, walks away from her school, her head held low. Other students stare or whisper. She clutches her books tightly, a single tear escaping. She finds herself in Aunty Lucy's house and is in the sitting room seated by the window and listless.

Auntie Lucy tries to coax her to eat, her expression a mix of sternness and sympathy. Naomi does not look her way but sheds tears.

"But Naomi, you can't continue like this without food in this condition. You must eat to have the energy to sustain the stress of your new condition." (Naomi is not responding as she looks on.) "If you don't eat, I may have to force you to eat, I don't want any troubles on my hands." Naomi does not look her way.

Later, as night falls in Aunt Lucy's sitting room, Naomi is sick and vomiting. Auntie Lucy is there, holding her hair back, cleaning up after her, with her face etched with worry and a sense of duty.

Months have passed and Naomi's pregnancy is now very prominent. Auntie Lucy is teaching her how to knit or sew baby clothes, and there's a quiet moment of connection.

Naomi is learning the hard lessons taught by the pains of teenage pregnancy; and Auntie Lucy, despite her earlier anger, has become her nursing mother. She becomes Naomi's unwavering support system throughout the difficult months.

Naomi is resting on a mat while Auntie Lucy is preparing some fruit for her. Sasha, one of the neighbors, walks to the place looking grave.

"Auntie Lucy! Naomi! Have you heard?"

Aunt Lucy turns, sensing trouble, "Heard what my sister?"

"It's about that boy, Luciano. The one who…well, you know.?"

Naomi sits up slowly, her eyes wide with a mixture of dread and a tiny, unwanted flicker of hope. "Luciano? What about him?"

Sasha shakes her head, and with a tone that's a mixture of gossip and pity, says, "They say he's gone. Left the country. Someone saw him at the airport. Word is, he's gone to America. To study, they say. Further his education." Her words hang in the air.

Naomi stares at the neighbor, her face paling. The small flicker of hope dies instantly, replaced by a profound, crushing despair. "America!" she thought, "he had run so far away, to a different continent, to build a new life, while I am here, carrying his child, my own life in ruins."

Auntie steps forward, her voice sharp, "America? So, he runs away from his responsibilities, does he? Leaves this child to face the world alone, while he goes off to better himself. The coward!"

Naomi, whispering, with tears welling up, "He... he didn't even write. Not a word. He never asked about.... about me or the baby."

She looks down at her swollen belly as the finality of his abandonment hits her with full force. All hope she might have secretly harbored for him to return, for him taking responsibility, vanishes.

Auntie goes to Naomi, her anger giving way to a fierce protectiveness. "Don't you waste your tears on him, child. He's not worth it. We don't need him. You are strong. We will manage."

But Naomi can only stare blankly, with the news confirming her deepest fears. She has lost all hope in him.

>>>>>>>>>>>>>>>>>>>>>>>

Naomi, though young and pregnant, begins to work with community members and finds a new resolve. The initial despair begins to transform into a quiet strength and determination. She finds strength in community services and communal interactions.

In the community garden, Naomi, her pregnancy very heavy, is working tilling the soil or watering plants alongside other women. She moves with effort but determination. The women are singing as they do their community service job; and everybody is enjoying the interactions.

Mama, an elderly woman, sees Naomi helping in sweeping her compound, like her earlier community service but now with a different, more mature gravitas.

Though young and facing the daunting prospect of single motherhood, Naomi found an inner strength she didn't know she possessed. She refused to be defined by her circumstances, throwing herself into work and community service, earning respect through her courage and hard work.

She did not hide in shame but actively engaged with her community, working hard to support herself as best she could. She threw herself into public service work, and despite her situation, she becomes a known and respected figure for her diligence and helpful spirit.

Finally, the day has come, and Aunt Lucy helps Naomi from the house, who is under the pain of childbirth. They are followed by Sasha who is bearing a bag stuffed with items for Naomi.

Auntie told Naomi, "Be strong and soon we will get to the health center. Your child is ready to be born."

Sasha encouraged Naomi, "Be strong child. Your baby will soon arrive. We shall find someone to take us to the health center," as they helped her away from the house.

After Naomi has put to bed and is returning to Aunt Lucy's house carrying me…baby Nora. Sasha is bearing her belongings.

Naomi is looking a bit uncertain of what is next as she looks around the place where other neighbors are already gathered to await their return.

She looks at the baby in the arms of Auntie Lucy, and then one of the women takes me from Auntie Lucy and raises a happy ululation to welcome the newborn.

Another neighbor picks up a can of talcum powder from a low stool and puts some on Naomi's chest area and then takes some in her hand and puts it on her face and chest area too.

The other women start to take the powder and put it on their faces and chest areas. Suddenly someone raises a local song and the whole place erupts in a sonorous atmosphere of joy and excitement as the baby goes from one woman to the other in great admiration.

My mother Naomi, little more than a child herself, had no idea how to raise a child. It was a case of a child raising a child. Her auntie, my great-aunt Lucy, became our rock, helping to raise me, caring for both my mother and me with unwavering dedication.

Naomi walks out from the house trying very hard to calm and rock me to sleep who is crying so hard. The more Naomi tries, the more I cry. Naomi is getting frustrated and Auntie Lucy steps out from the house and takes me from Naomi and starts to rock me gently.

Auntie tells Naomi to go inside and rest her body. "I will make her sleep."

Naomi looks at Auntie appreciatively, "Thank you Auntie Lucy."

Auntie replied, "You are welcome my child."

Naomi walks into the house as Lucy starts to sing a lullaby to me and I start to quiet down.

Later that night, in the deep of the night, while the house is dark and quiet; Naomi was trying to stop me from crying relentlessly.

Suddenly, we could hear sounds of shouting and commotion from outside as robbers were operating in the neighborhood. Naomi is terrified.

Naomi whispers frantically to me, "Shhh, my baby, please shhh. Please stop crying. They'll hear you. Oh, please, please be quiet."

I continue to cry, piercing the silence of the night; and Naomi glances fearfully towards the window, imagining the worst.

"Baby, please stop crying. I don't want these robbers to break in here and harm me or take you away from me."

Her voice is now trembling, tears streaming down her face. "Oh God, please protect us. Please keep us safe. Don't let them find us. Make my baby stop crying, please!"

I continue to cry, and Naomi feels a wave of hopelessness wash over her. A single tear escapes her eye, rolls down her cheek and drops on my cheek and immediately I stop crying, to the relief of Naomi.

"What? You...you stopped!" A wave of relief so profound it's almost painful, washes over her. She pulls me into a tight hug, burying my face in my baby blanket. She's sobbing now with gratitude instead of terror and whispering to me, "Thank you. Oh, thank you, my sweet baby."

"Thank you, God," you answered my prayers.

Auntie Lucy comes from her bedroom to join them, "She stopped crying".

"Miraculously Auntie," Naomi replied.

Auntie said, "I am sure she is going to sleep now. Go into your room and I will be here to monitor what those robbers are up to. Go, take her in."

Naomi takes me into their room as Auntie Lucy sits by the window to listen to the shouts outside.

As time passes, Naomi, looking older and more careworn, has been trying to sell some small items on the street, with me strapped behind her back.

At the end of the day, Naomi is found in Aunt Lucy's sitting room trying to read a book by a dim lamp, but she's exhausted and keeps nodding off. She tries to stay awake but is overpowered by sleep. She puts her head on the table and naps off.

The next day, Naomi is found doing hard manual labor with others in the community garden, doing farm work or carrying heavy loads, with me strapped to her back.

Luciano, my father, was still nowhere to be found. My teenage mother struggled daily to raise me. The dreams of education for herself and then for me seemed to slip further away.

In those early years, I could not go to school. Even with the unwavering support of my mother's auntie, life was not easy for us. Then, one day word came…my father had resurfaced.

When I was about 12 years of age, I was outside in front of Aunt Lucy's house playing with Naomi who was now twenty-six. An older Auntie Lucy is seated and watching us as Naomi teaches me how to weave a sweater dress. Naomi looks tired but resilient.

Sede, one of the villagers, hurries to our place and is excited. "Naomi! Auntie Lucy! Have you heard? Luciano is back!"

Naomi freezes, her eyes widen, and a complex mix of emotions flits across her face. There is shock, old pain, and a flicker of something unreadable.

Naomi speaks in a voice that is barely a whisper, "Luciano? Back? Here?"

Sede replied, "Yes! Just arrived, they say! He came back from America. With a Master's degree, no less! A big man now!"

Auntie Lucy looks grim, her expression hardening at the mention of Luciano's success. "A Master's degree, is it?" she said, "and what good will that do for the child he abandoned?"

I'm looking from my mother to Auntie Lucy, sensing the tension and not understanding the words but feeling their weight. Naomi continues to stare, the news of Luciano's return, and his apparent success, sinking in.

The life she has scraped together for us suddenly feels even more fragile. Naomi slowly looks at me, a new uncertainty in her eyes. >>>>>>>>>>>>>>

Naomi, holding my hand tightly, stands before a house slightly better than Aunt Lucy's, but still modest. This is where Luciano is staying.

She takes a deep breath and knocks. The door opens and Luciano steps out. He is older, dressed in smarter clothes than before, and carrying an air of education and travel. He looks surprised to see Naomi, and then his eyes fall on me, his daughter. His expression is hard to read.

Luciano greeted her, "Naomi, it's been a long time."

She replied, "Yes, it has. This...this is your daughter." She gently pushes me forward a little.

I look up at this strange man with curiosity and a little fear.

Luciano looks at me again, a flicker of something - surprise? regret? - in his eyes. He quickly masks it.

Lucy, a mature lady, appears in the doorway behind him. She's well-dressed and is looking at Naomi and me with open suspicion and disdain.

Lucy asks, "Luciano, who is this?"

Luciano turns to Lucy with a strained smile, "Just an old...acquaintance, my dear, and her child."

He turns back to Naomi, his tone becoming business-like, "I hear you've been struggling. I'm back now. I want to help. I want her," nodding at me, "to live with me. I can provide for her. Send her to school. Give her a better life."

Naomi is shocked, "Live with you...and her?", as she glances at the hostile girlfriend.

"Naomi," he says, "she'll be well taken care of. It's the least I can do. I want to do what's right for my daughter."

Naomi looked at me, then back at Luciano and his girlfriend. She's feeling torn. The promise of sending me to school and of me having a better life is a powerful lure, but the thought of handing her child over to this man who abandoned her, and to this unwelcoming woman, is agonizing.

My father has a new life and a new woman, Lucy. Yet he asked my mother to let me live with him, promising to take good care of me and, crucially, to send me to school.

In the sitting room of Luciano's modest apartment, I'm scrubbing the floors and washing dishes, clearly treated like a house-help rather than a daughter.

Lucy oversees me with a critical eye, scolding me for small mistakes as Luciano looks on. "Now be careful with those," she says, "your wretched mother can't afford that in all her life. And be fast with that cleaning as we can't keep at that for the whole day." I continue working in silence.

One morning I was standing in front of Luciano's house watching other children in the neighborhood walking to school in their uniforms. Luciano steps out of the house. He is going to work.

I stopped him, taking his hand and he is surprised as I looked into his face.)

"Nora," he said, "What is it now? What do you want to say?"

I asked him, "Are you really my father?"

He looked shocked, "What kind of strange question is that? What made you say that?"

I was staring longingly at the other children dressed up in their school uniforms going to school.

Luciano followed my gaze to also look at the children, with a slight light of understanding briefly lighting his face. Then it disappeared under a cloud of guilt, confusion and anger.

I said, "These children are all going to school. They have fathers." I turned to look at him straight in the face, with tears welling up in my eyes. "Why does my father not send me to school like the other children? I am just like a child maid in my father's house."

He looks at me looking confused and is thrown off balance and lost for words. "You'll go to school soon ... I..."

Suddenly we hear the harsh voice of Lucy that pierced through and cut us off. I released his hand and hurried into the house, and Luciano used the opportunity to escape.

Living with my father and his girlfriend was not the better life my mother had hoped for. I was treated more like a servant than a daughter, and the promise of school remained unfulfilled.

My father was present but distant, often preoccupied or leaving the house for work or business. He rarely interacted with me directly, and when he did, it was brief and impersonal. Lucy was the one who primarily directed me.

I was sweeping outside of the house when Naomi walked up. As soon as I saw her, I stopped what I was doing and ran to jump on her excitedly. Naomi looked me over and saw I was not looking happy.

I said, "Mommy you came to see me?"

"Yes, my child. How are you doing?"

"Mommy, you can see that I am not doing well. I am suffering here."

Naomi looked around the place, her expression growing increasingly concerned as she could see the signs of my neglect and servitude.

She pulled me close to herself, her voice gentle but firm, "My child, tell me the truth. Are you happy here? Are you going to school like he promised?"

I looked at her, tears welling in my eyes, as I shake my head "No" silently. Naomi's face hardened with anger. She stood up just as Luciano and Lucy entered from outside looking gay.

Naomi turned to Luciano, her voice trembling with fury, "You lied to me! You promised you would send her to school! You promised you would take care of her! She's nothing but a servant in this house! Just look at her, so emaciated."

Luciano became defensive and annoyed, "Now, Naomi, don't be dramatic. She's fine. School takes time to arrange…"

He scoffs, "She's ungrateful, that's what she is. We give her food and a roof over her head."

Cutting him off, her eyes blazing, Naomi says, "I'm taking her back! She's my daughter, and I won't let you destroy her spirit like you tried to destroy mine!"

"Come and pack your things," Naomi said as she took my hand and pulled me towards the door."

Luciano steps in front of her, with his face contorted with rage. His educated veneer has vanished. "You will not take her! She's my child too! If you take her from me, I swear…I'll forever forget about you two, and she will be a cursed child! Nora, if you follow your mother, you will be worthless in life! All you'll ever be is every man's wife! You'll be a prostitute! That's my curse on you if you follow your mother!"

He points a shaking finger at me; an innocent child caught in the crossfire.

Naomi gasps, horrified. She shields me, pulls me behind her, and glares at Luciano with utter contempt and defiance. "Your curses mean nothing, you pathetic man!"

"Come, my child," as she changed her mind from going into the house, turns and walks away, pulling me with her, leaving Luciano and his fuming girlfriend behind.

The terrible words of the curse hung in the air. My mother, furious at the broken promises and my mistreatment, took me away. My father's response was not remorse, but a terrible curse, words that would echo in my heart for years to come.

My mother was now a grown woman, and I was a teen. The memory of my father was distant, but the words of his curse...those I kept locked in my heart. When I became a teenager, I took this very seriously and told myself that I would never have children with any man until I was married.

I'm looking at my reflection in a small, cracked mirror, a thoughtful, determined expression on my face. I turn from the mirror and pick up a Bible.

I remember, "Worthless? Every man's wife? A prostitute?", there's a flicker of pain and then steely resolve in my eyes.

"No. I will not be affected by his hatred. I will not let his bitterness define my life. I will be the best of myself. I will prove him wrong."

I looked at my mother. Naomi, who is mending clothes with a needle. A look of deep love and respect passes between us. I make this vow, "I will never have children with any man until I am properly married. I will not repeat the cycle. I will build my own future, on my own terms." I opened the bible, sat beside Naomi and started to read silently.

//PART TWO:

THE WEIGHT OF RESPONSIBILITY

Later, my mother got married to another man, who is my siblings' father. I was the only child from my mother's first relationship and the oldest of eight children overall. In an African setting, being the oldest means you become like a second mother. My daily job was to take care of my siblings. My mother has remarried and is living with her new husband and seven children.

Our home is humble but clean.

>>>>>>>>>>>>>

This is where life took another turn and I have come to live with David, my stepfather, and seven "would be" siblings.

Suddenly, I was the oldest of eight. In our culture, that came with a heavy responsibility.

Mr. David, my mother's new husband and my stepfather is a kind man with seven young children from his previous marriage. I, as a teenage girl, stand beside my mother, already looking responsible and a bit burdened. The family unit is large and clearly a handful.

One day I was in front of David's house helping my siblings with their chores, as David and Naomi watched silently in admiration. I became a second mother, sharing the burden of caring for the younger ones with my mother.

My own teenage years were quickly overshadowed by the needs of my new, large family. I was surrounded by the younger children and already stepping into a role of significant responsibility with a grueling daily routine.

My days began early around 5:00 AM, filled with the responsibilities of bathing my younger siblings, dressing them for school, packing their lunches, and ensuring they were all taken care of.

After dropping them off at school, I would rush back to the marketplace to buy groceries, prepare meals, clean the house, and wash laundry – all before heading to school myself.

My school started at noon, and I faced a daunting walk of 45 minutes to an hour to get there. This routine became my life for five days a week, and through it all, I learned invaluable lessons in multitasking and time management.

From the living room of David's house, I would wake up in the dim light of dawn, already looking tired. I would move to wake the younger siblings, making sure that all are properly awakened, and I would make everybody kneel for morning prayers.

Outside of David's house, I would bathe the younger children, one after the other, and send them into the house to take the next person. There is a kerosene lamp standing to light up the early morning darkness. I dress them for school, combing their hair, and tying shoelaces.

Then in the kitchen, I would cook and dish out the food and pack lunch packs, a mountain of small food containers. I set them up and took them batch by batch to the sitting room. I would lead the seven little ones out of the house with their school bags and lunch packs and walk them to school from the compound.

I would then go to the market and shop for groceries, while haggling with vendors and navigating the paths in the market carrying my shopping bag.

I would return home to begin the chores of cooking meals over a simple stove, washing the dishes and cleaning up the kitchen, cleaning the house, sweeping, scrubbing, and doing laundry by hand, a large pile of clothes.

>>>>>>>>>>>>>

Once done with my chores, I walked the dusty, rural road under the midday hot African sun to my school, carrying my school bag. The walk is clearly long and arduous. It was finally time for my own education, but even that was a struggle.

I had to walk between 45 minutes to an hour, every day at 12:00 PM, just to get to school. Five days a week, under the scorching sun or through seasonal rains, I made that journey. The desire to learn and to be more than my father cursed me to be, fueled my steps.

Growing up as a hardworking young girl, much like my mother before me, I developed the art of multitasking with ease. It wasn't a choice, but a necessity for survival and for clinging to my own dreams of an education.

My mother, wanting a better chance for me, managed to send me to a boarding school. She paid for my first year's tuition, a significant sacrifice for her.

It was a new, larger, but still modest boarding school building. The first day, I was standing out front with Naomi, with my school box and bag, as we talked in my new environment.

We see other students walking about and into the school. Naomi looks proud but also a little sad to be sending her daughter away. She hands me a small bag with my belongings.

"Nora," she said, "this is a good chance for you, my daughter. Focus on your studies. Make me proud."

I replied, "I will, Mama. Thank you for this." We went into a passionate mother and daughter embrace and shedding tears; and Naomi helped me with my box into the school.

For me to continue and succeed in my education, I had to work doing menial jobs like cutting grass, to help support my tuition. Every shilling earned was a step towards the success of my education.

Inside the school, I was sitting up on my narrow bed in a sparse dormitory, shared with other girls. It's late. I was reading a letter by the dim light of a shared lamp. My face shows a mixture of emotions - happiness at hearing from home, but also a touch of loneliness.

During all my time in boarding school, my mother wrote to me only once. That single letter became my most treasured possession. She never visited, neither did my stepfather, not until I graduated from junior high.

In that solitude, I became devoted to my Bible and my God. My faith became my constant companion, my source of hope and resilience.

I carefully folded the letter and put it away safely. Then I picked up a well-worn Bible, opened it and began to read, finding solace and strength in its pages.

The move to high school took me to the neighboring city, where I was determined to complete my education and to build that future I so desperately wanted. But fate had other plans.

I was walking to school, now being in a high school. The atmosphere was initially normal, with students going to classes. But then, a sense of unease began to permeate the scenes.

People look worried, news is spreading in hushed, anxious tones. Sounds of distant unrest, perhaps sirens or shouting, began to filter in. Suddenly, chaos erupts. People start to run in the streets. There are sounds of gunfire or explosions in the distance.

//PART THREE:

CIVIL WAR

Students are fleeing from the school, panic on their faces. I was caught in the throng, looking scared and confused. It was then that the brutal civil war broke out in Liberia.

My academic dreams, so close to being realized, were abruptly cut short. From the sanctuary of school, we were suddenly fleeing for our lives, running from the rebels. I ran with other students, looking back in fear. The dream of education is replaced by the nightmare of war.

As the conflict escalated, my family and I found ourselves fleeing from the rebels. My mother and my siblings sought refuge in the city where I was attending school, desperately escaping the chaos that engulfed our homeland.

Luciano is sitting in front of his house with a transistor radio which he is keenly listening to for news. Lucy is seated nearby too, and some neighbours are also seated with them. The atmosphere is tense.

Reports are coming in of a major rebel incursion. The National Patriotic Front of Liberia, the NPFL, led by Charles Taylor, has launched an attack from the territory of Cōte d'Ivoire. Their stated aim...to oust President Samuel Doe. Heavy fighting is reported.

Luciano spoke, "Lucy, this is it. We have it, a war on our hands. Hey. They want to turn us into refugees in this country.

On the roads, there were men, women, boys, girls and children escaping from the troubled areas with their little loads. Some have their little ones on their backs and on their shoulders. There was a trail of escapees. He went and worked with the Ministry of Education for some time during the Civil War.

After he came to America and got his master's degree in education, he lived in Liberia for some time. He was still there when I was coming to the United States; Shalom and I went and met him in the capital to say bye to him. He died in 2017.

At David's house, there are some modest-sized loads sitting outside the place and Naomi is standing and keeping the seven children of David from straying away as they wait for David to join them from the inside.

He walks out with his transistor radio to join them. He says, "We have to get going."

Naomi asked, "Where to?"

David replied, "We shall follow the others to escape to where these sounds of death are not heard. We may go towards Nora's school area."

Naomi, "Good, that is a good suggestion, so all of us can move together."

David hands his radio to one of the boys, as they pick up the loads and step away from the house.

When they arrive in the city, they find streets which are now visibly affected by war, some buildings damaged, people looking scared, and a sense of tension and danger everywhere.

I was standing alone, trying to find a safe place or information, and looking lost and frightened. Suddenly I heard my name called.

It was Naomi's voice calling out desperately, "Nora! My daughter! My daughter!"

I turned to see Naomi, my mother, running towards me. She looked exhausted and terrified.

I cried out, "Mama!" as we ran into each other's tight embrace, holding on to ourselves.

"Nora, we had to leave. The rebels... they were coming to our village. We came to find you. We have to stay together."

"Mama, thank God that you were able to run away from the village. How about father and the children?"

Naomi replied, "They are somewhere in a local school with others that escaped from other places. I came to search for you, so we can stay in one place as a family."

"Mama, there is fear in every mind now and the towns are getting deserted. The school has been vacated and deserted. I will get my bag and will go with you. Let's go now." We walked away from there, holding on to each other.

My mother and my siblings, while also running from the advancing rebels, came to find me in the city. In the midst of war, our family was reunited, but our safety was far from certain.

Despite the war, some semblance of life tried to continue. In the city where we now lived as refugees, we tried to attend make-shift schools, being extremely careful not to get into any trouble with the rebel army personnel who mounted checkpoints.

On the road near a rebel check point, I was walking along with my younger sibling, David, Jr. We are well dressed, which now makes us stand out. As we approached the rebel checkpoint - armed rebels, some very young, looked menacing.

They also had some other civilians whom they had intercepted. One rebel yelled, "Hey, stop and come here." With my eyes wide in fear, I stopped with David Jr. and waited in answer to the rebel soldier.

I asked, "Sir?

The rebel eyed us suspiciously, "Where do you think you're going dressed like that? You government officials' children, trying to escape, eh?"

Terrified, I replied, "No, sir! We are just students. We live nearby. Please, we mean no harm."

The rebels laughed mockingly, shoving me and David Jr., and pointing their guns threateningly. Other captured civilians were nearby, looking on in fear.

"Students? Or spies?", he said, "we'll see about that. Maybe a lesson is in order for those who support the government."

David Jr. asked, "Sir??

A second rebel spoke up, "What is 'sir'? Join the rest over there quickly." I looked at my brother as both of us joined the rest of the civilians that had been intercepted by the rebels.

It was a tragic experience for myself and my brother as the rebels mistook us for the children of government officials. They threatened our lives, believing we were trying to escape the violence.

In a horrific twist, we were forced to participate in the execution by the gunshot of another innocent person, which left us terrified and traumatized. We were coerced into joining the crowd of other captives, and as fear gripped us, we were ordered to strip out of our clothes. The rebels were wearing red, and I was also wearing a red dress, which made my situation even worse. I took off my dress right there on the road, leaving me in just my bra. I was crying and trying to hide myself alongside my brother.

In a moment of pure panic, I found myself in only my sleeping bra, crying and desperate as I clung to my brother.

David Jr. and I found ourselves being led along the road by rebel soldiers, along with some of the other civilians held by the soldiers. We were stripped of our clothes up to our chests. I was in my sleeping bra and my top is on my shoulder as we marched along, terrified with the others. Most rebels were jeering.

One older rebel soldier seemed uneasy with the humiliation. After a little walk, he commanded the trail to stop. Looking at the group of captives, he pointed at me, "You and you," (also pointing at David Jr.) "step aside here." We obeyed and stepped aside from the rest, fearing the worst. "The rest can go."

The other rebel soldiers saluted him and led the rest of the captives on. The rebel turned to me and David, raising his gun. He said, "Now come with me!" while pointing to the bush. "Go!"

David and I start to cry as we walk into the bush with the rebel soldier following behind with his hand raised.

We see the rest of the captives and the other soldiers still walking along. The captives are looking terrified and hopeless as they trailed along the road with the rebel soldiers threatening them with death.

Meanwhile, in an abandoned school refugee camp, David gathered with Naomi and six of his children. They are looking deeply worried, as they expectantly look ahead in hope of suddenly seeing me and David Jr. returning home.

Naomi is sobbing quietly as David Sr. looks straight ahead in silence. Then he starts to pray, "Father, you have given us a promise of deliverance in times of our troubles. We are in the middle of that trouble right now. Come to our help."

Naomi said, "Amen."

"The wicked has driven us from our homes and now our offspring are missing from us. Father, I pray that you keep Nora and David safe wherever they may be. Send your angels to be their guides, in Jesus' name.

Naomi said again, "Amen."

David Jr. and I walked to a spot in the bush with the rebel following with his gun. "Stop!" he said, "and turn around."

We turned around and faced the rebel, with great fear written all over our faces as we kept our gazes on him.

He said, "What do you want me to do to you now?"

"Have mercy on us," I said, "we are but innocent children who was returning to join our family, before we were taken yesterday. Our father is not a government official but a church pastor."

Narrowing his eyes, he said, "Really? Both?"

I said, "Yes sir, please have mercy on us." There was a long-drawn silence from the rebel as he kept his steady look on them. Then he sighed a loud one. Then he said, "Now run!"

David Jr. asked, "Sir?"

"I said run!", he said, and don't ever look back!"

We turned and started running away from him, glancing back.

He watched us, raised his gun, aimed at us, steadied his gun, and put his finger to the trigger to shoot…but then lowered his gun, turned and walked away from the bush.

Naomi is in the refugee camp surrounded by David's children. They are waiting and looking as they wait hopelessly for the return of David Jr. and me. Naomi is shedding tears as she holds the children together.

Slowly, she goes on her knees to pray, and the children also do the same. Naomi said, "Father in heaven, we are your children. Please help us in this time of our troubles."

The children started screaming, "Nora, Amen! We see Nora and David Jr. coming!"

Naomi opens her eyes and seeing Nora and David, jumps to her feet and runs into an embrace with them. The siblings also do the same.

Naomi, "My children! You are safe?"

I said, "Yes! God saved us from the captivity of the rebel soldiers!"

David Jr. said, "Where is father?"

Naomi replied, "They took him away to fight."

David cried out, "What? Papaaa…"

Naomi said, "There is danger in this land, we have to find safety, by all means. We are no longer safe here. Others are moving, we must move with them. We have to escape with the rest to Côte d'Ivoire."

>>>>>>>>

For days, we hid from the rebels, living in constant fear. The situation was dire, with young and strong men being forced to fight, and young girls taken as wives for the rebels.

My mother, recognizing the grave danger we were in, made the difficult decision to escape to a nearby country, Côte d'Ivoire. We eventually made our way to a refugee camp in a town called Tabou, where we sought safety amid the ongoing turmoil.

>>>>>>>>>>>>

In a crowded, squalid "Internally Displaced Persons" (IDP) camp in Tabou, there was a group of girls and women, listening to a young woman named Tilda, a Survivor, recount her horrific experiences. Her voice is low and haunted.

"They came to our school to hunt for us, and they kidnapped and dragged us out. So many of us were molested." She shudders, with tears in her eyes.

The others cried, "Heeei."

Tilda, "They... they did terrible things. Multiple fighters raped us. Yet after all the sexual abuse, they then gave me to a commander. His wife...he called me wife. I was only fourteen."

The listeners are horrified by the story as they listen silently. Some shed tears, in an atmosphere of shared trauma.

The stories were everywhere, each more horrifying than the last. Girls were abducted from schools, from their homes, and from IDP camps like this one. They were subjected to rape, gang rape, and sexual slavery. Many were forcibly assigned to commanders as wives and endured years of unimaginable abuse. That 14-year-old survivor story was just one of countless tragedies.

I looked around the camp, at the faces of other girls and young women, wondering how many of them carried similar scars, visible or

invisible.

In the IDP camp in Tabou, outside a makeshift shelter, Naomi is seated with me and my siblings around her as they share some pieces of bread with jugs of water to fill their stomachs.

Naomi is cutting and handing small portions of bread to the children, and they are sharing water from a sizeable water can as they eat pieces of bread in their hands.

Naomi said, "Nora: This is all we can get for everybody for now. We will eat it and drink enough water to fill our stomachs. We have to go and find more food so that the children do not die from hunger.

Naomi holds me to herself and starts to shed tears. I'm not left out as she brings all the siblings together and they all bunch together to cry together, "Oh God of mercy and compassion, please come to our help."

Naomi's resilience and strength during this time was incredible. She shielded us as best she could from the worst of the war impact, always putting our needs before her own.

I, in turn, tried to support her, to be the responsible older sister to the rest.

"We will get through this, my daughter," Naomi said, "we have to believe that. We have each other."

I said, "I know, Mama. We will."

Naomi, "Besides I believe that the God of the Heavens and the Earth is with us. He will never fail us. He will see us through all this and finally reunite us with David, my husband." The strain is visible on both their faces.

As for my stepdad, God kept him, and he is still alive at the time of this writing. He and four of my siblings still live in Liberia, and one of the siblings live in Minnesota, USA.

The camp is a place of desperation and simmering tensions. The camp in Tabou is overcrowded and conditions are basic. Aid workers (UN, NGOs) are present distributing food, water, and medical supplies. That's how life was in the refugee camp - no employment, nothing at all. We had to pay rent while being unemployed. During that time, my mother, my siblings, and I had to garden and sell the crops so we could survive.

In the refugee camp, life was difficult. Many days, we went without food, had nowhere to sleep, and could not afford our rent. The United Nations would come once a month and provide us with two cups of rice and one cup of beans, expecting that to last a whole month for each family.

Naomi and I were standing in the relief queue to get palliatives. We got the supplies and left the queue with them. Naomi said to me, "I have to take what we have gotten home to the children while you stay back a little to see if you can get more. But do not delay to come back to our shelter."

"Okay Mama," I said as Naomi turns and hurries away with the supplies, and I stayed back to wait for luck to show up for extra supplies.

//PART FOUR:

LOVE, MARRIAGE AND COST OF FAITH

By the corner, a young man is seated and is reading his bible while he waits on his turn for the supplies.

I strayed to where he was seated, and he looked up to see me. "Hi," he said, I'm Daniel."

I asked him, "What are you reading?", and he lifted the worn-out Bible to me.

He said, "My Bible. The only thing that gives me strength and hope."

I exclaimed, "Hope! Here?"

He said, "Especially here, yes.", and a moment of understanding passed between us.

Daniel and I walked together, talking about faith and our dreams. He preached to a small group in the refugee camp while I watched, with admiration. I saw Daniel give his only meal to a starving child, and my admiration deepened.

Back in the IDP camp, while Naomi was there with all her children, she pulled me aside, looking worried.

"Nora," she said, "he has nothing to offer you. No money. No home. A marriage built on faith alone. But faith is enough." Naomi sighs as if she is not convinced.

Later, as Daniel and I sat under the stars, silence hung between us.

Daniel said, "I have nothing to give you. No money. No house. Just my faith...and my love."

I told him, "That is enough."

Things were difficult inside our cramped temporary shelter in the refugee camp. A single, flickering candle or a small oil lamp provided meager light. Naomi is trying to mend some clothes while the younger children are asleep.

Nora is looking out through a small opening in the tent/shelter, at the vast, dark expanse of the camp, dotted with other faint lights.

Years began to pass in the refugee camp. Each day was a struggle for survival, but also a testament to human resilience.

We were safe from the bullets, but not from hunger, disease, or the gnawing ache of displacement.

I ask Naomi softly, Mama, do you think we will ever go home?

She pauses her mending, looks at me with a sad smile and says, "Of course we will. I pray for it every day, my child. Home is not just a place, it's...it's where our hearts belong. We must keep hope alive. One day, the war will end." I nodded at her with a somber expression.

The camp, with its endless rows of tents and the constant hum of thousands of displaced lives, feels like a permanent reality. The daily routines in the camp were a lesson in patience and endurance.

Queuing for hours for basic necessities was a normal part of life. Water, food, medicine, and everything was precious, and often insufficient. I learned to be resourceful, to make do with a little.

I saw my mother do it, and I learned from her. We were survivors. In my early life, God blessed me with two very strong women and one good friend who were there for me with love and support at crucial times. At the time of this writing, my mother Naomi, Aunt Lucy and Abigail have long ago passed in Liberia, but they will forever live in my heart.

In an open space, Daniel and I are seated and having a discussion under the moonlight.

"I am thinking of leaving this part of the world." I said to him, "I want to travel to Ghana with my friends."

Surprised, he threw a quick look at me, "Ghana? Why?"

I answered, "My cousin says there are jobs in Accra. Not great ones, but something. Anything is better than this." as I gestured around. "Two cups of rice and one cup of beans for a family unit for a month? We deserve more than just surviving.

Concerned, he asked me, "What about your mother? Your siblings?"

Resolutely but with a hint of guilt, I said, "I'll send money back when I can. Maybe eventually find a way to bring them too. But someone has to be first, to find a path out."

"What about me? About us?" he asked.

"Daniel, we shall plan about ourselves as we grow."

He said, "You think this is the right thing to do now?"

I replied, "I think it is going to be good for us and our families."

He said, "Just as we are coming to know each other and you are planning to run away?"

"I am not running away; I am trying to make things better for all of us."

He said "Well…"

Many young girls turned to prostitution because they could not endure the hardship and wanted to survive. However, as a young teenager, I refused to live that life. I had decided to live my life for Christ alone and wait for my husband.

I stood up, resolved, as my friends gathered their few belongings. We looked toward the camp exit, toward an uncertain future but potentially better than our present.

I stayed in Ghana for two and a half years. It was hard work, but different from the camp. I was able to earn a little, save a little, and dream of something more.

But my thoughts often returned to my family still struggling in the refugee camp. It was time to return home, to say goodbye to my mother and siblings properly.

I had new plans now - to continue traveling through West Africa, hoping to eventually find my way to America. To a place where I could build a real future, not just survive.

>>>>>>>>>>>>>>>

Naomi and I sat in front of the makeshift shelter that harbored our family, as we discussed. Naomi, looking concerned said, "Nora, America? That's so far. And dangerous for a young woman alone."

Determined, I replied, "I need to find opportunities, Mama. For all of us. I can't stay in this camp forever."

Naomi looked at me with a mixture of pride and worry. She sees the determination in my eyes, and the woman I have become despite all the hardships.

Sounding resigned but supportive, with a sigh, Naomi said, "You are always strong-willed. Like me. Just be careful and remember who you are. What about Daniel?"

"He has a plan too. Will see him in church tomorrow," as Naomi and I embrace ourselves passionately.

There was a modest church in the refugee camp. The service is in progress. I was sitting in a pew, dressed in my best, but simple, clothes. The church was full, and during the service, I noticed the young man leading the congregation.

In the pulpit is Daniel, passionate and charismatic, leading the service. When our eyes met there was a connection. "Even in our darkest hours, God has not abandoned us. Even in this place of waiting, of hardship, of anxiety, He has a purpose for each of us."

Members, "Amen!!!"

Daniel, "He will not abandon us."

Members, "Amen!!"

Daniel, "He will make a way for all of us to get to our desires."

Members, "Amen!!!"

Outside the church, we see the congregants trooping out after the service ended. I walked out and waited outside as the rest of the people are leaving.

While walking home with my siblings and mother, the lead minister came running after me and asked, "Hey, Moira, how are you? I haven't seen you in a while. Are you dating anyone?" I found the question surprising and asked him why he wanted to know. He replied, "Oh, I just wanted to know because you've been away for a while."

Curious, I asked him who sent him to ask me. When I looked behind him, I noticed the young man I had seen leading the service standing there. I told the minister, "If he wants to know anything about me, tell him to come and meet me himself."

Shortly after, Daniel walks out from the church and looking around briefly sees me standing and walks up to me. We hug briefly and start to talk.

"Nora, you came to church service."

I replied, "That was a powerful and inspiring sermon you gave. I was greatly encouraged."

He said, "I am happy you were able to attend the church service. Thought you were too tired to attend because of your journey back home yesterday."

"I can joke with everything," I said, but not my commitment to my Christian life."

Later, during an open-air event, we met again, talked for a while, and eventually started dating. I prayed to God, telling Him that I did not want to engage in any sexual activities unless I was married. I asked for a sign to confirm whether this man was truly my husband, and that's exactly what happened.

Daniel, "Thank God that you came back."

Me, "I came to get ready for more travels."

Daniel, "I have a good news for us."

Me, "Say it to my ears. What good news?"

Daniel, "I have an opportunity to travel to America for studies. It is an opening for asylum seekers, and I have the window of opportunity."

Me, "That is a good news indeed. My return was actually to start a wider travel of the African states to see if I can find an opportunity to finally go to the U.S."

Daniel, "Can you see now, how God orders the footsteps of the righteous? What you desire is right at our arm's length. One of the conditions is that one must be married to completely qualify for this opportunity."

Daniel, "Is anything stopping you from getting married? Will you marry me?"

I was silent as I kept my head down, and as Daniel watched me, unsure of what would happen next)

Daniel, "Nora? "

I raised my head slowly to look at him, drawing a smile.

"Yes Danny, I will marry you"

Daniel, "Oh praise the Lord! Right away I am going to see your mother to make this official."

Me, "And then?"

Daniel, "Without any delays we will get the church to formalize the union."

Me, (Aflutter) Danny, thank you for this. I can't wait to tell this news to my mother."

Daniel, Lets go there immediately, so you can get her blessing.

Naomi was already agitated, "A penniless minister? This is who you want to marry? A man who can barely feed himself?"

Unbeknownst to me, the young man came from a background where he had little experience in relationships.

Defensively but with understanding, I said "He's a good man, Mama. Kind, faithful, devoted to God."

She expressed doubt about my fiancé, pointing out that he only had one shirt and one pair of shoes, and that he had previously been told by other girls that they were not compatible.

Emotionally, Naomi said, "You are my firstborn! I had such hopes for you. You were going to America, going to find a better life, help lift this family up! How did you just abandon your tall dreams? You know I was against this union from the onset."

Taking my hands in hers, her voice softening but still urgent, she continued, "There are other men, good men with means who could have provided for you, for all of us. Why choose to lack and struggle when you could have security?"

Gently but firmly, I said, "What if I married a rich man who pulls me away from my faith? Money isn't everything, Mama."

I felt a quiet conviction. "I see him for who he is, not what he has. I believe God has brought us together. Daniel has a bright future with his plans to move to America to continue with his education."

With tears in her eyes, Naomi said, "You are just like me when I was younger, stubborn to a fault." (shaking her head) "I pray you won't regret this choice, my daughter. This night you move in with your husband, away from me and all your siblings to your new home.

I embraced her, my own eyes filling with tears.

My mother was very upset and disappointed, crying because I was the oldest daughter, and she had expected me to marry someone who could take care of us. She said, "You are like a mother to your siblings."

I understood her concern but wanted to marry someone who would not take me away from my faith. Her approval meant everything to me, but I could not let it determine my path.]

After a little time, we decided to get married. We had no money, and the church helped arrange the wedding.

On the wedding day, Daniel led me out from the church dressed in my wedding gown. He is dressed in a simple suit.

We are followed by Naomi, my siblings, the ministering Pastor, some church members, friends, well-wishers and a photographer. We all stood to pose for wedding photographs, and the photographer clicks away.

I prayed to God, telling Him that I did not want to engage in any sexual activities unless I was married. I asked for a sign to confirm whether this man was truly my husband, and that's exactly what happened.

The peace I felt, the connection we shared - it was my answer. So, I got married to Daniel, though he had nothing to sustain us as a family, but we had faith that things would turn around for us especially as he had an opportunity to travel to America to study in the near future.

Unbeknownst to me, the young man came from a background where he had little experience in relationships.

Inside Daniel's single IDP camp room, on our first night as a married couple, the makeshift room is clean but extremely sparse. A single candle provides dim light. I am sitting on the edge of the makeshift bed, looking nervous but happy. Daniel bent over and planted a kiss on my lips, and I smiled. Feeling shy but happy, I said, "So... this is our home now?"

Looking around, Daniel said, "It's not much, but it's ours. We'll make it better with time. Anyway, this is an IDP camp, we do not need so much here.

I felt an awkward but sweet moment between us.

Then he glanced at the door, seeming distracted before saying, "I... I promised some of the brothers I would meet them tonight. To celebrate, just for a little while.

I was surprised but tried to hide my disappointment. "Tonight? But... it's our wedding night."

Trying to reassure me, he said, "I won't be long, I promise. They're waiting for me. It's tradition, you know? The men celebrate together."

I nodded slowly, not wanting to argue on our first night as husband and wife, but clearly felt hurt and confused. "Softly I said, alright. I'll wait for you here."

He kissed me again and then left as I remained sitting on the bed, alone. The door closed and my smile faded as I looked around the empty room. The reality of my new life began to sink in.

On this our first night after getting married, he left me at home to hang out with his friends, which was very difficult for me. It was the first indication that marriage might not be what I had imagined and that my husband might not be who I thought he was.

>>>>>>>>>>>>>

After a few months, I was pregnant, sitting outside and looking ahead and tired. I was spitting intermittently. Daniel walked out from the room to leave for the day.

Feeling weak, sitting on our only chair, I asked, "Do you think you might be able to find some food today? We're down to our last bit of rice."

Sounding frustrated, he said, "I've been trying. You know I've been trying. There are no jobs in this camp. Everyone is struggling."

Holding a hand on my big belly, I replied, "I know. I'm sorry. It's just... I'm so hungry all the time now. And the baby..."

His voice softened as he knelt beside me, "I know. I'm worried too. I'll try again today. Maybe the church can help us. Our little one needs to be strong." He touched my belly gently.

Just then, one of our neighbors came, a kind-faced woman holding a small bowl and smiling. "I made too much bean cake this morning. Thought you might like some. I felt such gratitude and relief.

Daniel looked both grateful and ashamed because of the charity. He said earnestly, "Thank you. Thank you so much. God bless you."

The neighbor handed over the bowl and left. I immediately took a small portion, eating slowly, savoring each bite, as Daniel watched with his expression pained.

We had no food to eat and lived in a single room. In addition to the challenges, I had a very difficult pregnancy. We were eating cake for breakfast, lunch, and dinner because we had no other food, and neither of us was working, with no other source of income.

Each chapter of my life was filled with struggles, yet they have all contributed to the person I am today—someone who deeply understands the power of faith, love, and community support.

While I was pregnant in the refugee camp, I had to be on bed rest for most of my pregnancy to keep the child safe. With poor nutrition and no food to eat, I was hungry all the time.

From the very first day of my pregnancy, I had felt unwell. The nausea was relentless, and I suffered from severe vomiting. I remember the feeling of my stomach churning and the overwhelming sense of discomfort. I was frequently forced to urinate, and on many occasions, I found myself unable to control it, which added to my distress.

As the days turned into weeks, I experienced an intense hunger that I had never known before. Despite the life within me, I felt as though I was simply fading away.

Life in the camp was incredibly difficult, and my mother witnessed my suffering firsthand. We were living in overcrowded conditions, and there were times when we had to share a cramped space with others. We eventually had to move in with a pastor and his family during the middle of my pregnancy because our living situation became untenable. Throughout all of this, my mother stayed by my side, supporting me and my siblings as best as she could.

I would walk slowly through the camp, pregnant and weak. I stopped at different neighbors' homes, receiving small portions of food from each one. Some gave me sympathetic looks, and others seemed slightly annoyed but gave anyway. I accepted each offering with profound gratitude.

We lived on the charity of neighbors as my husband was unable to secure any work. Whenever our neighbors cooked, they would share a portion of their meals with me.

One of our neighbors, Sharon, handing me a small container of food said, "Here, child. It's not much, but it should help a little. How are you feeling today?"

Accepting the food with trembling hands, I said, "Thank you, thank you so much. I'm... managing. The baby moves a lot. That's a good sign, isn't it?"

She said with a nod, "Yes, that's good. Strong like its mother."

Again, I said, "Thank you for the food." Then I moved on to another neighbor's dwelling.

Verna said quietly, "We're all struggling here. Your husband should be taking better care of you."

Despite my hunger, I was defensive, "He tries. There's no work. He goes out every day searching."

I continued with my daily rounds, a ritual of survival. My face showed the strain of depending on others, and of never knowing when or what I would eat next.

I was grateful for every bite, but I worried constantly about my baby being born under such malnourished conditions. I ate not when I wanted or what I wanted, but when I was given whatever neighbors cared to share.

While lying on the bed, I was looking extremely ill and dangerously thin except for my big belly. I was sweating and periodically rushing to a bucket in the corner to throw up. My husband was sitting beside me, helpless and frightened.

Between bouts of nausea, my voice was weak. "I've never felt hunger like this. It's like I'm being eaten from the inside. And vomiting... I can't keep anything down."

Daniel, wiping my forehead with a damp cloth, said, "I'm so sorry. I've failed you. Failed our child."

Suddenly clutching myself, I said, "I need to... again…" He quickly helped me to the bucket where I retched painfully, though there was little to expel. Then I collapsed back onto the bed, exhausted.

Daniel said, "It is well."

Whispering, I replied, "I'm afraid. What if something happens to the baby? What if something happens to me?"

Daniel took my hand, with his voice breaking, "Don't say that. You are strong. Our baby is strong. We have to believe that God will see us through this."

I nodded weakly, wanting to believe it, and suddenly, I was seized by another urgent need. I felt embarrassed. "I need to... the urination... again." He helped me up once more, this time to another corner where a makeshift toilet was set up.

The pregnancy took a terrible toll on my body with severe nausea, vomiting, frequent and uncontrollable urination all made worse by malnutrition. There were moments when I truly believed I was dying slowly, my body unable to sustain both myself and the growing child within me.

Outside of Naomi's camp shelter, she was seated and reading the Bible with some of the siblings. I walked to the place looking weak.

Naomi saw me and quickly hurried to me. As she helped me to sit down, her face was lined with worry. The siblings watched with concern.

Naomi looked distressed, "Look at you! You're wasting away before my eyes!" She said to Samuel, "Bring some water for your sister quickly!" Samuel hurried to bring water which I sipped gratefully.

I tried to sound strong, as I said, "I'm alright, Mama. The baby is still kicking. That's what matters."

Angry and upset, she said, "Alright? You call this alright?" gesturing at my frail body, "This is exactly what I feared! Where is he? Where is this husband who can't even feed his pregnant wife?"

Defensively, I said, "He's looking for work, Mama. He tries every day."

Bitterly, she said, "Trying isn't enough when your wife and unborn child are starving!" (Her voice broke) "My firstborn child, reduced to this..." She turned away, wiping tears.

I reached out to touch her arm. I said softly, "Please, Mama. Don't be angry with him. It's not just us, everyone in the camp is suffering. Besides, no matter the condition, I am grateful I am not every man's wife. The curse is broken."

Naomi turned back to me, with her anger giving way to maternal concern. She sat beside me, putting an arm around my shoulders.

Gently she said, "Yes, you are not every man's wife. I'll share what little we have. You and the baby need strength. (Looking around at the cramped shelter)

It's not much, but you're welcome to stay here if things get worse."

I leaned against her, grateful for her support despite her disapproval of my choice. My mother witnessed my suffering firsthand, and it broke her heart. She did all she could to support me, but life in the overcrowded camp was unbearable for everyone.

Back at Daniel's shelter room, I was sitting on the bed, with my pregnancy now very advanced. Daniel sat beside me, and we had an intimate conversation.

Daniel said thoughtfully, "We should start thinking about names for our child. Something meaningful, something that reflects our journey."

Placing a hand on my belly, he said, "Despite everything we've lost - our homes, our possessions, our security, we still have our faith. We still have hope for the future."

Taking my hand, he said, "What about 'Shalom?' It means peace."

Smiling, I tested the name - "Shalom." Nodding I said, "I like it. Peace is what we all long for in our country, in our lives."

Placing his hand on my belly, he said, "Shalom it is, then. Our little beacon of peace in a world of chaos."

We shared a moment of connection, both feeling the baby move beneath our hands.

Softly I asked, "Do you ever wonder what kind of world our child will grow up in? Will Liberia ever know true peace again?"

Answering with conviction, he said, "I have to believe it will. And even if the world around us remains broken, we can create peace within our family, within our home, wherever that home may be."

I leaned against him, drawing comfort from his presence and his words. Suddenly the first pang hit me, and I yelled out, holding my waist, "Whaaaaat???"

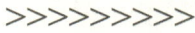

I told him to hurry to Mama's shelter and urgently call her to come immediately. "I think that Shalom is about to arrive."

Suddenly in panic, he said, "Hey, okay, just be strong," and dashed out from there as I was groaning under the pang.

Delivery was a long process. I was in labor for close to 24 hours. I was forced to give birth in my mother's room in the refugee camp because many of the other women who went to the hospital during that time would die. My mother was afraid for me and did not want me to go to the hospital because of the high infection rate.

So, I was forced to give birth at home. The delivery lasted for 24 hours because the umbilical cord was wrapped around my daughter's neck. She almost died when she came out; she was all green until one of the helpers reached inside to check on the baby. They found out that her neck was trapped in the umbilical cord, and they had to unravel it before I could finally give birth.

In front of Daniel's shelter, he was standing and pacing anxiously with the senior pastor of his church and some male neighbors.

Daniel and the rest of the men outside were engaged in fervent prayers for me as they continued to hear my cries from Naomi's shelter.

Daniel said, "Pastor, this labour is taking too long - since yesterday's night and she is still yet to deliver."

"Keep praying," Pastor said, "the Lord will see her through. Keep your faith alive."

The women were inside the shelter taking charge of my child's delivery, as I was crying out in agony, "Mama! It hurts so much! Something's wrong, I can feel it!"

Daniel reacts and stops praying momentarily to listen.

Naomi was encouraging me, "Be strong, my daughter. You can do this. Push when the midwife tells you."

The midwife, exclaimed concerned, "The cord...I can see it! It's around the baby's neck! We need to work quickly!" she said to the helpers.

Naomi was talking to me, "Breathe child...just breathe. God is with us. He will not abandon us now." I was screaming in pain.

Daniel is seriously affected as he looks at the pastor for assurance. Pastor said, "Midwife, Child of God keep praying and faint not!"

Urgently the midwife screamed, "The baby is turning green! I need to untangle the cord now!"

Moments of intense fear and activity follow. Then finally, the cry of a newborn baby filled the air!

Daniel caught the senior pastor in an embrace and then turned to the others, embracing them emotionally; and then broke down in tears as we hear the women inside the shelter lift up their voices in praise!

Naomi, "Praaiiiiise the Lord!!!!"

All, inside and outside, "Haaaleluyaaa!!!"

Daniel, with raised voice, "Shalom is here!"

>>>>>>>>>>>>

However, life did not get any easier after Shalom's arrival. We faced a new set of challenges, as there was little food for me and even less for my newborn. I often found myself prioritizing my daughter's needs, sacrificing my own nutrition to ensure she had enough to eat. Raising an infant in a refugee camp, where resources were scarce and opportunities even scarcer, felt like an insurmountable challenge.

There were many challenges of raising a newborn in the overcrowded, resource-scarce refugee camp including:

1. Cramped Living Space: I had to bathe baby Shalom in a small basin while other camp residents move around in the confined space.

2. Water Line: Waiting in a long line for water, from a large water tank. Baby Shalom is strapped to my back, the sun beating down mercilessly.

3. Makeshift Clinic: I was holding a feverish Shalom, waiting anxiously among many other sick refugees for medical attention. It is a relief medical team for the refugees.

4. At nighttime, walking with a crying Shalom, trying to soothe her without disturbing the many others sleeping nearby in the crowded camp.

5. Food Distribution Line: Standing in line for food rations. Shalom now a bit older, is still on her back as people push and shove around.

Every ounce of my strength and resolve was tested. Clean water, medical care, adequate food, and even basic privacy were all luxuries we could rarely afford. Yet somehow, through God's grace and the support of our community, Shalom grew and was a bright light in our difficult circumstances.

I sat in front of Daniel's camp shelter with Shalom who was now a toddler, playing with a simple toy made from scraps. Despite the harsh surroundings, there was a moment of joy between mother and child, a testament to resilience and love in the face of adversity.

//PART FIVE:

WALKING THROUGH FIRE

Eventually, my husband received an opportunity to travel to the United States for a job and educational scholarship. He left us behind in the refugee camp, and it was over a year before we could reunite. In the meantime, my husband was limited by his student visa and was not allowed to work. I, too, faced restrictions since I did not have work authorization. To survive, I took on odd jobs like babysitting and braiding hair. I would travel from family to family, looking after their children while my own daughter was by my side. It was a grueling routine, but it was for our survival.

I continued my education in Warsaw, Indiana, after we moved to the states. I was a full-time Mom, full-time wife and a full-time student.

After two years, we moved to Chicago, where I became pregnant with our second daughter. Throughout my second pregnancy, I struggled to find stable work, continuing to braid hair and care for other children as best I could. In the midst of this, I joined a Bible study group for stay-at-home moms. It became a source of strength and community for me. One of the women in the group took it upon herself to teach me how to drive. Late at night, when her husband was home, she would take me to an empty parking lot and patiently guide me until I felt comfortable enough to drive on the highway.

When I gave birth to our second daughter, I faced yet another challenge. I was reluctant to wash her clothes in the public laundry machines, so I opted to hand-wash them at home. When my husband refused to help, I confronted him with his laziness, leading to a confrontation that escalated into physical. The fear and pain I felt after just giving birth left me feeling even more isolated and helpless.

Yet, even amidst all the struggles, I clung to my faith and the hope for a better future, determined to navigate the challenges of motherhood and life in a new country. I picked up the phone, my hands trembling slightly as I dialed the police. I had found myself in this situation before having to call the authorities on him for his aggressive behavior. This time, however, felt different, and I hesitated, unsure if I should proceed.

Instead, I reached out to an older woman from our shared homeland, someone I trusted. When I spoke with her, she expressed gratitude for my decision not to call the police. "Thank you, Moira," she said, "I will talk to him for you." It was a small comfort, but it felt like a lifeline in a sea of chaos.

This marked the first instance of physical abuse I experienced from my husband, just three days after giving birth. The emotional and mental torment I had endured leading up to this moment had escalated into something far more dangerous. For so long, I had hoped for a happy and stable family, pouring every ounce of my support into him as he pursued his education for over eight years. Despite never having a job myself, I became the breadwinner, supporting our family during his academic journey. I babysat our children and managed our household, all while he focused on his studies, backed by the family insurance I provided.

After he graduated from Moody Bible Institute, we made the decision to move to Warsaw, Indiana, where he wanted to pursue his master's degree in divinity. Every relocation we undertook seemed to revolve around his aspirations, with little regard for my own needs or desires. It was as though my existence was secondary; his goals took precedence, and I was merely a supporting character in his narrative. Our lives were dictated by his choices, and I felt increasingly invisible.

Throughout our relationship, he never encouraged me to seek my own personal growth or education. Instead, he seemed to view my ambitions as a threat, as if we were competitors rather than partners. He had promised that once he graduated, I would have the opportunity to pursue my own education. However, when that time came, he refused to support me, and instead, we found ourselves moving again, this time to a different location that suited his educational pursuits.

During this tumultuous period, I became pregnant again, this time with him working as a teacher. The pregnancy itself went smoothly, but when it came time for delivery, everything unraveled. The challenges began as soon as I entered the delivery room. I was given an epidural, but it did not take effect as intended; rather than numbing my lower body, it sent a wave of discomfort up into my chest.

I called for the attending nurse, and she promptly came to assess the situation. After a brief examination, she assured me that she would slow down the medication and fetch an anesthesiologist. However, I felt an overwhelming urge to stop the process entirely, fearing for my body and my baby.

"Please, just take it out," I insisted, sensing that something was terribly wrong.

As the medical team scrambled to address my concerns, I felt a sense of impending doom. This was just the beginning of a harrowing ordeal that would change my life forever. Despite the chaos, I held onto the promise I found in Jeremiah 29:11, believing that there was a divine plan for my future. I felt protected that night, knowing that my friends were praying for me as I faced the uncertainty of childbirth.

After the anesthesiologist arrived and removed the epidural, the doctor attempted to deliver my baby. I was determined to have a natural birth despite the complications. With every contraction, I pushed with all my strength, but the challenges did not end there. Once my baby was born, I faced yet another crisis—the placenta would not detach, and the medical staff had to intervene. As the doctor reached in to address the issue, I suddenly felt an overwhelming rush of blood. It was as if a faucet had been turned on, and I could see the room darkening around me. That was the last thing I remembered before losing consciousness.

When I finally opened my eyes again, I found myself in the ICU, surrounded by medical staff and my husband. He told me that he had stayed by my side throughout the ordeal, refusing to leave me alone even for a moment. However, I later learned that he had abandoned me in the ICU to attend church, leaving me to fight for my life without his support.

After my release, I faced numerous complications, including severe anemia and the necessity of blood transfusions. I underwent a traumatic surgery that involved the removal of my uterus and ovaries, a procedure that I never anticipated would be part of my journey

Recovery was a long and arduous process. I had to relearn how to care for myself and my children, grappling with the new reality of my health. I vividly remember a moment when my eldest daughter looked at me with concern and said, "Mommy, I can't see you being normal." I reassured her, "My baby, I promise I will be normal again, by the grace of God." I was determined to heal, but even as I struggled to regain my strength, my husband pressured me to return to work. He insisted that I needed to maintain our health insurance, seemingly oblivious to the toll that my physical and emotional exhaustion had taken on me.

// PART SIX:

CALLING AND PURPOSE

My husband became a pastor when our kids was about the ages of 15, 8, and 2 years old. The challenges of becoming a Pastor's wife were very challenging, but this was something that from childhood I always wanted to be.

I always wanted to be involved in the ministry. When I was a teenager, my friends from school and from church always used to call me "missionary". I was assigned in a choir, and we did mission work together, so this was like a passion of mine to always get involved in ministry and to become a Pastor's wife.

As challenging as it was, I still enjoyed it. I taught the Women's Bible study at times, and I taught a little Bible study group also in our apartment. The kids used to play the piano sometimes in church, and the kids were also involved with him in the ministry.

In the midst of all this turmoil, I found myself wrestling with the stark contrast between my hopes for a loving family and the harsh reality of my circumstances. I had endured so much for the sake of my family, but I was beginning to realize that the cost of that endurance was too high if it meant sacrificing my own well-being. As I sat in quiet reflection, the harsh reality began to surface: the man I had once called my husband did not love me. This realization hit hard, especially given the sacrifices I had made, including enduring a traumatic experience that was akin to a scene from a dramatic film.

After giving birth and undergoing extensive surgery, I had hoped for understanding and support, yet he seemed more focused on pressuring me to return to work than on my recovery. With a heavy heart, I confronted him, saying, "I don't think you really love me." I firmly refused to comply with his demands to go back to work, knowing the physical and emotional toll I had just endured.

I had to relearn basic functions, like walking. Each time I attempted to get up, even for something as simple as going to the bathroom, I would almost faint from the exertion. In my desperate state, I found myself back in the emergency room multiple times, grappling with the repercussions of my condition.

When I suggested taking legal action against the medical practice that had contributed to my suffering, he dismissed my concerns, citing our Christian beliefs and insisting that we could not sue. Out of a misguided sense of loyalty and my desire to be a faithful wife, I silenced my own instincts, even as I faced a heartbreaking medical reality: I would never be able to have children again, even if I were to remarry. Meanwhile, he was free to later start anew, remarrying and having two children with his new wife.

// PART SEVEN:

THE CRACKS BEGIN TO SHOW

As I continued to navigate life in Warsaw, the cracks in our marriage became increasingly evident. For an entire year, we lived under the same roof, yet we were emotionally and physically separated. The emotional abuse escalated, morphing into physical confrontations that only added to the torment I was enduring. He would hurl insults at me, belittling my appearance and my intelligence, verbally abusing me day after day. I tolerated this mistreatment solely for the sake of our children, hoping that my strength would somehow shield them from the chaos unfolding around us.

The early warning signs in our marriage began when we lived in Warsaw, Indiana. We had bought a cell phone together as a family phone and we were all on the same plan. At one point, my husband was working in a group overnight. When he started doing night shift, he became involved with one of his coworkers, so there was a time that I suspected some calls. One day I confronted him with looking at the phone, but he refused to give me the phone. Instead, he broke it in front of me.

Another time when I suspected that he was having something outside of our marriage, was with a female friend of mine that always used to call when I was at work. I was working the evening shift, and I would get off at 11. By the time I would get home it was after 11:30 to 12:00.

Every time I came home, I would see her name on the caller ID, that she was calling right about the time that the kids were already in bed. I questioned him on several occasions, and he told me that she only called for them to talk about politics and the stock market. I even confronted the sister and told her to please stop calling my husband in my absence; that she is my friend, not his friend. She still did not stop.

One night, I was jolted awake to find him looming over me, casting a shadow that filled me with terror. Fear gripped my heart as I recalled countless stories I had seen on television about individuals who were betrayed by their partners. I prayed for guidance, feeling an urgent need to remove myself from this volatile situation before it escalated further. My intuition warned me that I had to act, especially when he became physically aggressive in front of our children. That moment was a turning point; I knew I had to leave.

That very night, I took my children and sought refuge at a friend's house, staying in her basement for a few days. It was a brief respite, but when I returned home, I was met once again by the same monster I had tried to escape. Nothing had changed; the cycle of abuse resumed as if I had never left.

I would drop the kids off at school each day, then find solace walking around a nearby lake, desperately trying to find clarity and peace. But one day, after returning to my car, I unleashed months of pent-up emotion, screaming and crying until I could cry no more. In that moment, I resolved that it was time to take decisive action.

Before reaching this breaking point, I had sought counsel from a pastor who had married us years ago. He was a family friend, and I hoped he might provide some guidance. I explained my desire to leave the marriage and requested my share of our joint investments so that I could start anew. However, he refused, siding with my husband despite the injustices I had faced.

During the years when he was a full-time student, I had been the one working tirelessly to provide for our family, yet I was denied my rightful portion of our savings. While we lived together in separate rooms, my husband began transferring our investments solely into his name, liquidating our children's college savings and other assets without my consent.

The final straw came when I realized I had to escape for good. I packed up my children's belongings from our spacious five-bedroom home and prepared to leave. That night, as we huddled in the guest room, he took drastic measures, removing the doorknob and lying across the door to prevent our departure. Fear and frustration filled the air as my children struggled to sleep in the midst of chaos. The next morning, determined to leave, I called one of his good friends in New York, seeking assistance. After some convincing, he managed to persuade my husband to let us go, finally allowing us to leave that toxic environment.

We hit the road, heading from Warsaw, Indiana, to Ashburn, Virginia. After a long day of driving, we stopped for the night, exhausted but relieved to be free from my husband's grasp, even if just temporarily. Yet, my sense of safety was short-lived. He continued to pursue me relentlessly, often lurking in the shadows, waiting for the right moment to re-enter my life.

// PART EIGHT:

STRENGTH FOR THE STORM

When I finally decided to file for divorce, the situation became even more perilous. He grew increasingly volatile, trying to manipulate my emotions and finances, threatening to take away the very money I had earned to support our children.

As I navigated this tumultuous journey, I realized that the battle for my freedom and for the well-being of my children was far from over. It was a fight that would require not only courage and resilience but also a steadfast commitment to reclaiming my life and securing a brighter future for my family.

He dragged me through the courts, taking me on a tumultuous journey that spanned across three different states, each with its own set of challenges and heartbreaks. At the same time, he was swimming in the waters of North Dakota, where I was often left stranded, battling my own storms. In Indiana, where he made his home, and Delaware, where our divorce proceedings were taking place, the stakes were incredibly high.

I was fighting tooth and nail to gain custody of our children, a responsibility that weighed heavily upon me, especially since he consistently neglected their needs. It was a constant struggle; he outright refused to care for them, which left me grappling for funds to provide for our kids. The little money I managed to scrape together for their food had to be diverted to pay for lawyers, who represented me in various courtrooms across these states.

After our divorce, he remarried in about a year or two years, not exactly sure, but it wasn't long. When he got remarried, our oldest daughter was fifteen years old, the middle girl was about seven or eight, and our last child had just turned two years when I left.

It was about this time that another major storm hit us. My oldest daughter was diagnosed with a serious illness in her junior year of high school.

To make the challenge of the illness even more difficult, her father refused to acknowledge the illness. He dismissed it as just "attention seeking" in spite of how seriously ill she was.

To God be all the Glory, that at the time of this writing, my daughter has gained the victory over that illness.

The divorce itself was a long, drawn-out, and incredibly nasty affair. There were countless days when he would take the children on what he called "vacations," but in reality, those trips were often marred by neglect. He would refuse to feed them properly, taking out his anger on them instead. He particularly targeted our youngest daughter, irrationally blaming her for the collapse of our marriage.

It was painful to witness how poorly he treated his own children; during their visits, he would frequently withhold food. I found myself in a helpless position, having to send grocery money through various means, including using services like DoorDash and Uber Eats just to ensure they had something to eat. He and his new wife imposed a strict vegan diet on the kids, which they were not accustomed to, leaving them feeling starved and deprived. I would often send food multiple times during the vacations, just to ensure that they were not going hungry.

On top of this, when he would come to pick them up, at times they didn't want to go with him. He would sometimes resort to bringing law enforcement officers to forcibly take them from our home, causing them immense distress and heartache. Even while we were still living together, I tried to encourage him to build a relationship with his children, but he was resistant. It was as if he refused to acknowledge how profoundly the divorce was affecting them.

The emotional turmoil was so severe that we eventually had to seek therapy; they needed professional help to navigate through the devastating impacts of our split. The situation was truly terrible, and it felt as though we were all trapped in a nightmare.

>>>>>>>>>>

This man, whom I had met in a refugee camp, was someone I believed I could build a life with. I envisioned a future where we could create a nurturing environment, one that could serve as an example for other young couples who were enduring similar hardships.

I had seen the struggles of many in the camp, and I was determined to avoid falling into the traps of prostitution or other desperate measures just to survive. I said "no" to selling my body, even when faced with the harsh realities of life. Instead, I invested my hopes and dreams in our relationship, believing that we could create something beautiful together.

Throughout his educational journey, I was there to support him. I stood by him when he had nothing, and when he eventually earned his master's degree, he belittled me, calling me "small brain." His emotional, physical, and mental abuse took a toll on my self-esteem, especially as I worked tirelessly to support our family while he was in school full-time. He dismissed my efforts, labeling me a "workaholic" as if my commitment to our family was a flaw.

//PART NINE:

REDEMPTION AND NEW BEGINNINGS

Today, I share my story because I know there are countless women, including many wives of so-called pastors and ministers, who are enduring similar situations in silence. They suffer in silence, desperate to save their marriages while fearing the exposure of their husbands' dark secrets. Many are afraid that revealing the truth will lead to judgment or ostracization from their communities.

We brush these issues under the rug, pretending that everything is fine, and we hush-hush about the abuse we endure from these so-called men of God. But this is not the life that God intended for us, nor is it the plan He has for our children.

It is crucial for our children to see that it is not acceptable to endure such treatment, as they might grow up believing that this behavior is normal. It is absolutely not okay to suffer in silence or to continue to support men who abuse their wives while hiding behind the facade of spirituality. Sisters, I urge you to recognize that you have the power to make a change. You do not need to remain in a state of silent suffering. Speak out! God has a better plan for you, one that offers hope and a future. He desires for us to rise above the abuse and declare, "Enough is enough!"

This is not just about you; it's about your children and future generations. They deserve to live trauma-free lives, lives where they can thrive without the shadow of abuse looming over them. Victory belongs to us and our children.

My oldest daughter Shalom, despite a major medical crisis during high school, graduated from high school and went to college. She works in Human Resources hiring doctors for hospitals, and she gave me a grandson whose name is Adaan. Shalom is a very loving and caring person, who always has been there to take care of her siblings.

She was one of my strong backbones during the divorce after I left with her and her siblings. She had to watch them while I worked two jobs to keep the roof over our head. She's very inspirational to her siblings.

My second girl is Ade', who graduated from University of Delaware with a degree in

Psychology. She is a very intelligent young girl with a very bright future and very focused on life.

The last girl is Lelah, who is currently a junior in high school. She lives with me and is also very smart, intelligent and beautiful.

These are my three Precious little ones that the Lord has invested me with to bring them up in the way in which they should go, and they will not depart from it. I praise him for giving me the opportunity to be called their mother.

Shalom is the very outspoken one in the family, and Ade' is the reserved one who keeps to herself. She doesn't talk a lot, but she thinks a lot afterwards. Lelah is in the middle of the two of them, and she has a bit of each person's personality.

Please, my sisters, find the strength within yourselves to take a stand for your life. Break free from the chains of abuse. God is with you, and He will guide you towards freedom. Stand strong and break free in Jesus' mighty name.

// FINAL BLESSINGS

Before you close this book, I want to bless you:

May the Lord cover you with His feathers, and may you always find refuge under His wings. May every tear you've shed in silence be turned into a testimony of joy. May every burden you've carried alone be lifted by the mighty hand of God.

May you break free from anything that holds you captive — fear, shame, loneliness — and rise up into the fullness of who you were created to be. I pray God's favor surrounds you like a shield, and His peace rests upon your heart each day.

You are loved. You are seen. You are never alone.

Blessings,

...Moira Boakai

// ABOUT THE AUTHOR

Moira Boakai is a devoted mother of three daughters and grandmother to one grandson.

She is a faith-filled woman, and an inspiring voice for those who have silently suffered behind closed doors. Through her powerful testimony and unwavering trust in God, she has transformed her trials into a story of hope and restoration.

As the author of "The Diary of a Pastor's Wife", Moira courageously lifts the veil on the hidden struggles many women endure in silence; reminding readers that God is close to the brokenhearted and can heal even the deepest wounds. She continues to encourage, empower, and uplift others through her writing, ministry, and speaking engagements.

When she's not writing, Moira enjoys spending precious time with her family, praying for others, and sharing her journey to help women break free from pain and live in the fullness of God's love.

// BOOK OUTLINE:

PART ONE – *Our Beginnings in Liberia*

• A Child Raising a Child – My mother Naomi's beginnings, teenage pregnancy, abandonment by my father, and being cared for by my great-aunt.

• A Mother's Strength – My mother's resilience and public service shaped my view of strength and perseverance.

• The Absent Father Returns – Mu father's reappearance with a master's degree, his broken promise of education, and the curse he tried to place on me.

• A Daughter's Resolve – My determination to break free from his words and define my own future.

PART TWO - *The Weight of Responsibility*

• Becoming the Second Mother – Life as the eldest of eight siblings, the burden of caretaking, and growing up too soon.

• The Daily Struggle – Managing household duties before school, long walks to class, and the determination to succeed despite exhaustion.

• The Power of Perseverance – Lessons learned in resilience, survival, and self-sacrifice.

PART THREE - *Civil War*

• Loss of home

• Determination to survive

PART FOUR - *Love, Marriage, and Cost of Faith*

• A New Chapter – Falling in love, the dream of a godly marriage, and stepping into the role of a pastor's wife.

• The Hidden Battle – The struggles behind closed doors, balancing ministry expectations, and the silent suffering of a neglected wife.

• A Mother's Fierce Love – Daughter's illness, husband's denial, and my fight to protect and provide for our children.

PART FIVE - *Walking Through Fire*

• The Breaking Point – Choosing to leave, navigating single motherhood, and finding strength in God's provision.

• Working Two Jobs and Holding It Together – The relentless grind to keep my family afloat while ensuring your children thrived.

• A Father's Curse Broken – Watching our children graduate and succeed, proving every negative word spoken over you wrong.

PART SIX - *Calling and Purpose*

• Purpose and Faith Restored – Embracing my calling, sharing my story, and inspiring others with my testimony.

• The challenges of being a pastor's wife—expectations, pressures, and sacrifices.

PART SEVEN - *The Cracks Begin to Show*

• The slow unraveling of the perfect image—husband's neglect and emotional distance.

• Raising children under the weight of ministry expectations.

• The early warning signs that something is wrong in marriage.

• Another storm hits, my oldest daughter's serious diagnosis.

• Husband's refusal to acknowledge the illness, dismissing it as attention-seeking.

• Juggling work, caregiving, and holding the family together alone.

• The breaking point—the moment I realize I must choose between sanity and staying.

PART EIGHT – *Strength Through the Storm*

• The difficult decision to step away from marriage while still holding onto faith.

• Becoming both mother and father, working two jobs to support my children.

• Finding strength in my church community, friends, and God's grace.

• The emotional and spiritual toll, but also the quiet victories—watching my children graduate despite the odds.

PART NINE - *Redemption and New Beginnings*

• Daughter's healing journey, graduation, and the arrival of her grandson.

• The joy of seeing all my children succeed despite the past.

• The lessons learned through suffering and faith.

• A new chapter: peace, restoration, and a deeper relationship with God.